Woman Power

Published by **J. P. Tarcher, Inc.**

Los Angeles

Distributed by **Houghton Mifflin Company**

Boston

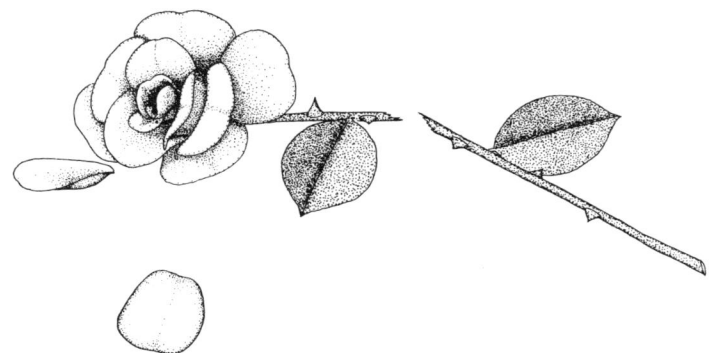

Mary Lou Brady,
Lucinda Dyer,
and Sara Parriott

Illustrated by Sara Parriott

Library of Congress Cataloging in Publication Data

Brady, Mary Lou.
　Woman power!

　　1. Women—United States—Anecdotes, facetiae, satire, etc.
2. Success—Anecdotes, facetiae, satire, etc.   I. Dyer, Lucinda.
II. Parriott, Sara.   III. Title.
HQ1420.B7　　646.7′0088042　　　　81-50007
ISBN 0–87477–173–0　　　　　AACR2

Copyright © 1981 by Mary Lou Brady, Lucinda Dyer,
& Sara Parriott

All rights reserved. No part of this work may be reproduced or
transmitted in any form by any means, electronic or mechanical,
including photocopying and recording, or by any information
storage or retrieval system, except as may be expressly permitted by
the 1976 Copyright Act or in writing by the publisher. Requests for
such permissions should be addressed to:

J. P. Tarcher, Inc.
9110 Sunset Blvd.
Los Angeles, CA 90069

Library of Congress Catalog Card No.: 81-50007

Design by Mike Yazzolino

MANUFACTURED IN THE UNITED STATES OF AMERICA

M 10 9 8 7 6 5 4 3 2 1
First Edition

*The authors dedicate this book to themselves.
They deserve it.*

Contents

Acknowledgements 8
Introduction 9

1. *Women Hitherto Hidden* 11
    Psst . . . 12
    Prepare Your Daughters to Make History 22

2. *The Big "O" Is Your Office* 25
    What Mother Never Told You 26
    How to Dress for Success 27
    The Job Interview 30
    How to Treat Your Boy 32
    Quiz #1: Rate Your Office 34

3. *How to Be on Top at Home* 37
    Four Basic Household Hints 38
    Cold Storage 39
    The Perfect Grocery List 40
    What's In the Medicine Chest and . . . 42
    Environmental Entertaining 43
    I Vant to Be Alone 44
    Quiz #2: Rate Your Apartment 46
    On Top on the Road 48

4. *Staying on Top of Attacks from the Bottom* 51
    Squelch 'Em! 53
    Offensive Statements 54
    Who Asked You Anyway? 56

5. *At Last, Men* **59**

You Must Meet the Most Fascinating Men   60
Where to Look   64
The Bicoastal, Out-of-Town, Always-on-the-Road Relationship   65
The 1980s Male   66
How to Buy a Man   68
What to Say to Your Mother Who Still Thinks You Should Get Married and Have Somebody Take Care of You   70
Quiz #3: How to Tell If You're a Female Chauvinist Pig   71
A Puzzlement   72
What Do All These Objects Have in Common?   73
Women Who Prove It Isn't So Bad to Stay Single   74

6. *If You Can't Join 'Em, Beat 'Em* **81**

Recreation   82
How to Be On Top of Your Leisure Time   83
Sportperson   84
Sportspersonship   86
Nobody Likes a Bitch   87

7. *You've Made It* **89**

The Nine Most Important People in a Successful Woman's Life   90
A Warning   91
Quiz #4: How to Tell if You've Made It   92
You Know You've Made It When . . .   95
Can You Do It Again?   115

About the Authors   127

Acknowledgments

The authors wish to thank the following men without whom this book would not have been possible:

Dan	Joe	Dick
Duncan	Lee	Larry
Andrew	Scott	Jack
John	Rodney	Rico
Brian	Jon	Bob

Introduction

Hundreds of books have been written on dressing for success, negotiating for power, and clawing your way to the top while never once losing your femininity. But, until now, no one has told you the real truth about what awaits you on that long sought summit of success.

Woman Power prepares you for all those dilemmas that mom and dad, the sorority, and even business school never even *mentioned*—how to reward your "boy" for a job well done, the dos and don'ts of shopping for a man, how to deal with a husband who's overspent on *your* credit cards, even what to tell your mother who thinks you should give up all this silliness and settle down.

Here at last is a book that destroys forever the myth that business for men is a piece of cake, while for women it's merely baking one. *Woman Power* is a manual for surviving and succeeding at success.

> If it had been up to Adam, we'd all still be naked in that garden.

Women Hitherto Hidden

1

Psst. . . .

If it had been up to Adam, we'd all still be naked in that Garden. Fortunately, Eve was a woman with a sense of adventure. When that snake slithered up and offered her a way out of all that Eden, she bit.

She was the first of a long line of unsung heroines, a few of whom are depicted here.

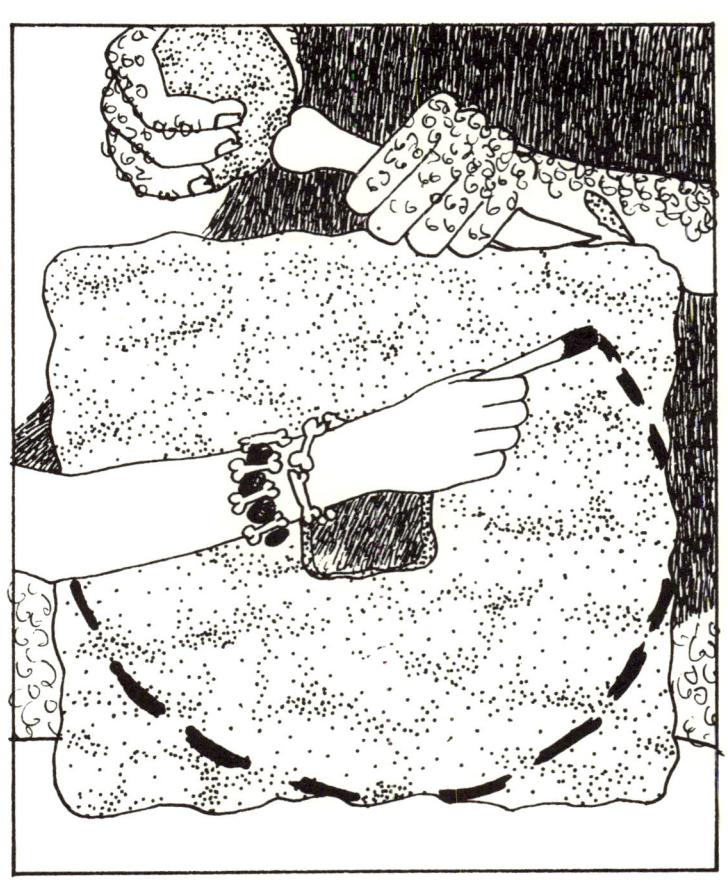

The inventor of the wheel

Mrs. Ben Franklin

The first Sassoon

Mrs. Isaac Newton

Discoverer of cooked meat

Mrs. Orville Wright

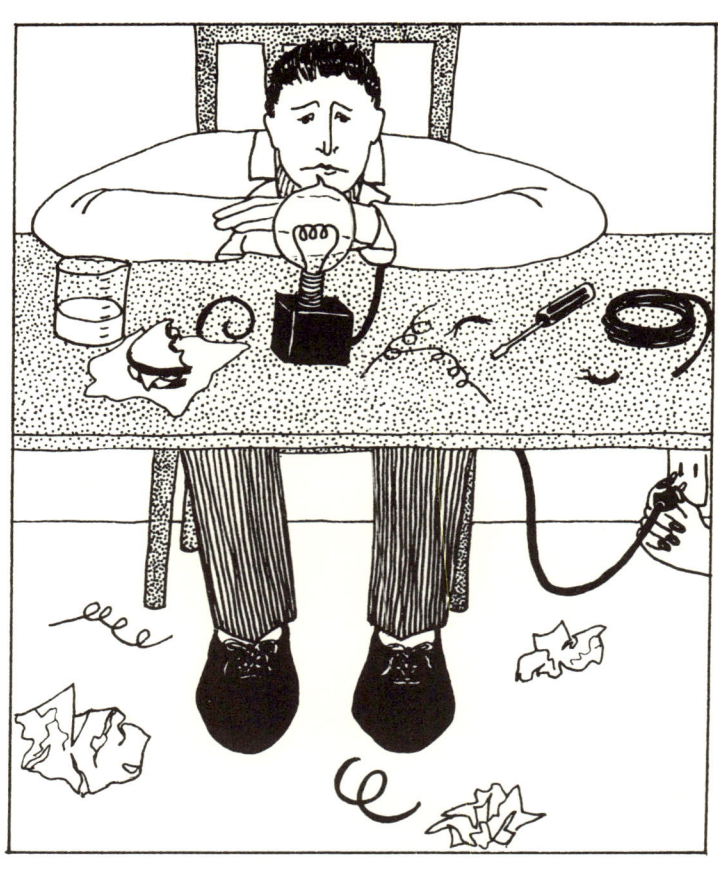

Mrs. Thomas Edison

The first assembly line

Prepare Your Daughter to Make History

No matter how nonsexist and liberal mom and dad claimed to be, it is likely that when it came to raising you and your brother there was a glaring lack of consistency. The truth of the matter is that your well-meaning parents overprotected you.

Your brother left the nest knowing how to fend for himself. You left with the illusion that "please" and "thank you" were the keys to success. Then you found out just how things *really* worked. What mother never told you was that when men say "after you" they may be planning to stab you in the back.

If you want to prepare *your* daughter for the real world, be cruel. Be hard on her. Let her know what to expect. These suggestions will help you point her in the right direction.

>Make her open her own baby food jars.
>
>Cover her teddy bear with sandpaper.
>
>Teach her to read with the *Wall Street Journal.*
>
>Get her a paper route in a ghetto neighborhood.
>
>Give her all her toys unassembled and without batteries.
>
>Give her chores like installing the hot tub and rotating the tires.
>
>Make her build her own bedroom furniture.
>
>Have her train the guard dogs.
>
>Give her the middle initials M.B.A. at birth.

"Tell them you're willing to relocate, don't tell them you'll have to ask your mommy."

The Big "O" Is Your Office

2

What Mother Never Told You

From the time he was big enough to sit on the edge of the bathtub to watch Daddy shave, your little brother was getting the message that men don their old school tie, pick up their briefcases, and go forth into the world to be successful. You, on the other hand, probably grew up thinking that being able to make the best fudge brownies in the neighborhood was the crowning achievement of a woman's life. Well, that may come in very handy when you are a den mother, but it won't do you a damn bit of good at General Motors. You've got to learn to play the game their way.

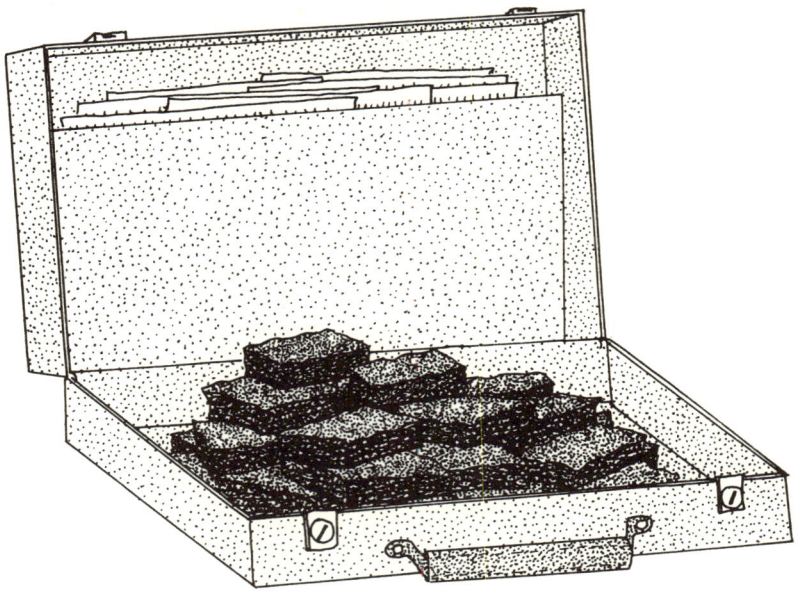

How to Dress for Success

*I*n the best of all possible worlds, the way you dress would have no bearing on whether you could do the job or not. You could walk through the door looking like Deborah Harry and still attain that great corner office with the southern exposure that you deserve.

Reality being what it is, however, men still run most companies. And, while they may look on a male employee who dresses like Gene Simmons as being "bohemian but creative," *you* they'll label a slob.

If you want to command respect and admiration, and foster the belief that you are management material, you better look the part. And looking good is almost as good as being good.

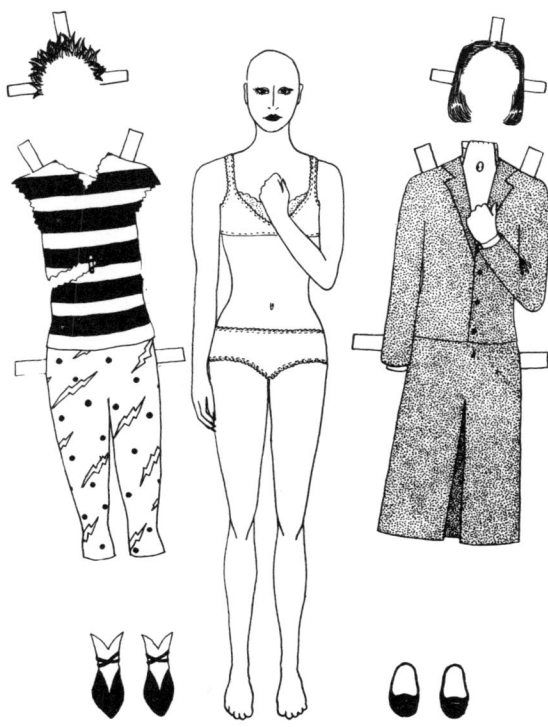

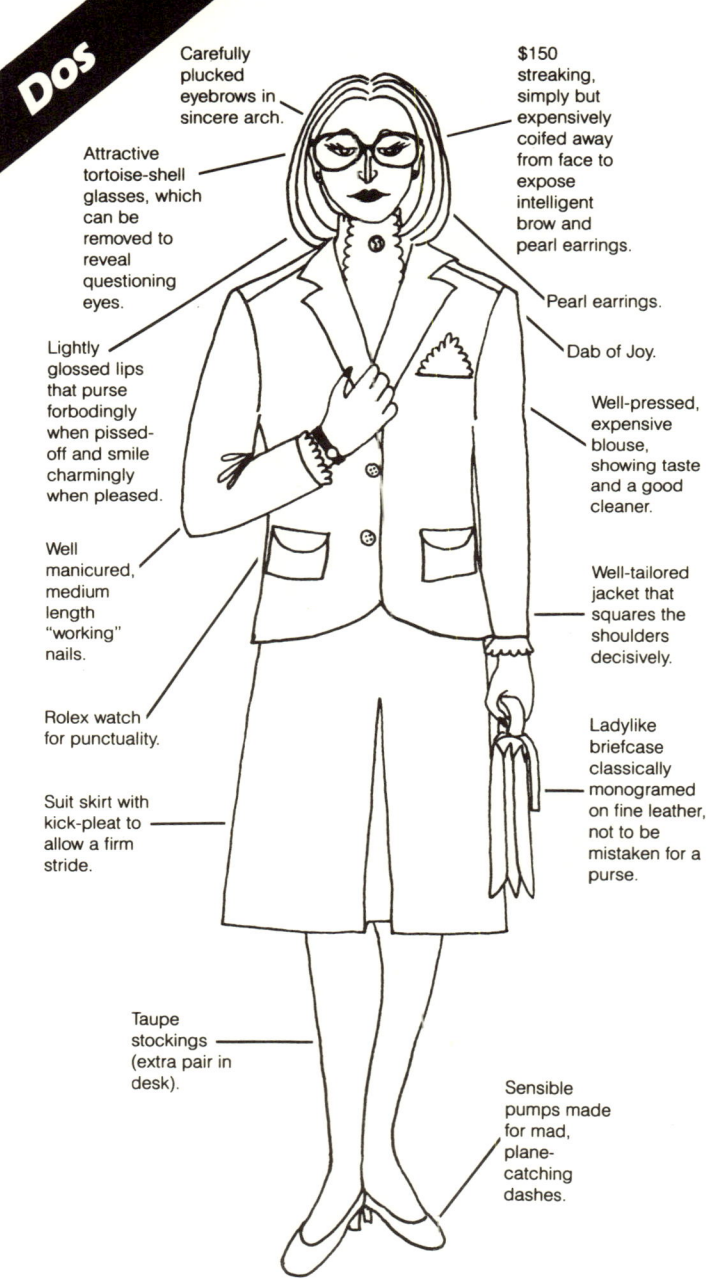

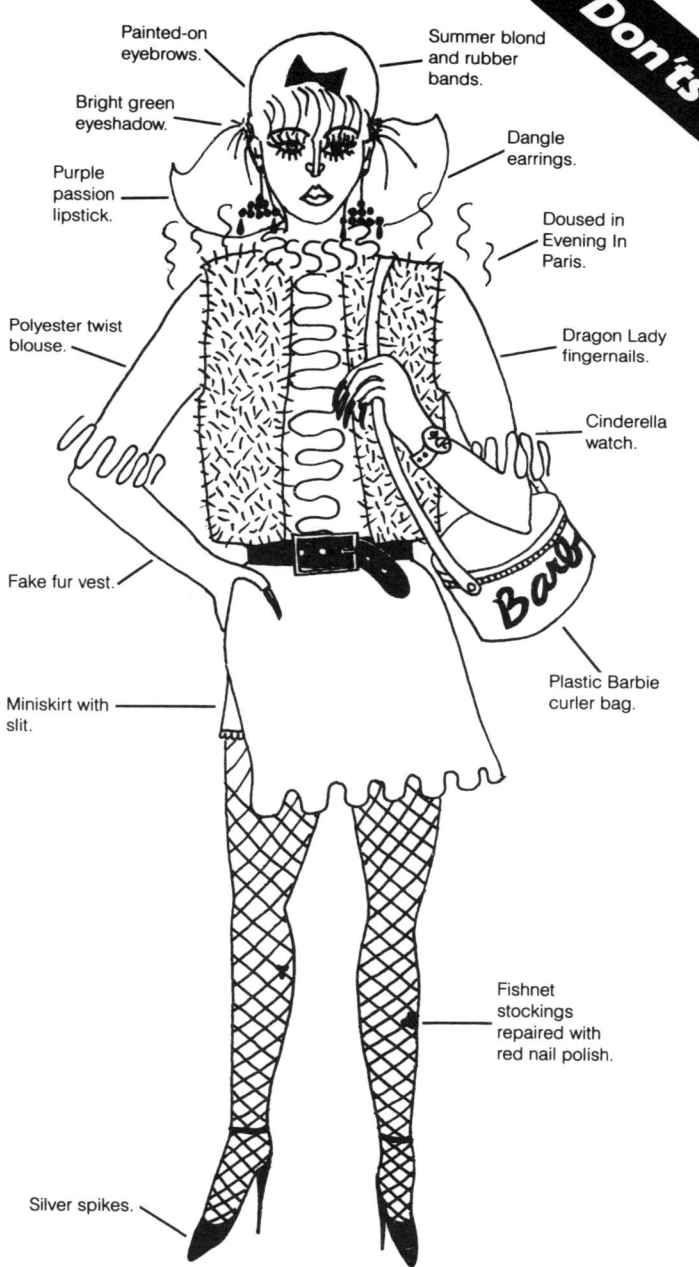

The Job Interview

Gone are the days when you put on a hat, pulled on a pair of spotless white gloves, practiced your most subservient smile, and went forth in search of a really great secretarial job. Today you can be interviewing for anything from drilling supervisor on an off-shore rig to team doctor for the Los Angeles Rams. You aren't going to be judged on your typing skills anymore, but there are still a few do's and dont's to observe.

Do bring a resumé.

Don't handwrite it on your Snoopy stationery.

Do wear navy blue.

Don't hug the cat for luck before you go.

Do pull your hair back.

Don't use rubber bands off the newspaper.

Do wear perfume.

Don't make it Jungle Gardenia.

Do arrive on time.

Don't park your Harley in the reception room.

Do have references.

Don't make it Bert Parks.

Do say you can start immediately.

Don't ask for Friday off.

Do know something about the company.

Don't mention the Senate investigation.

Do tell them why you left your last job.

Don't break down and cry when you tell them.

Do say you're willing to relocate.

Don't say you'll have to ask your Mommy.

How to Treat Your Boy

*A*t last. The big day has finally arrived. You've suffered the climb from being someone's "girl," to Administrative Assistant to the second vice-president in charge of word processing, to a responsible position that includes your own office and your own secretary. You hire a sweet young thing fresh out of Katie Gibbs and, boy, is he anxious to make good.

Men whose only previous supervisory positions have been as chief French fry cook at MacDonald's will handle this situation better than a woman if for no other reason than they consider it their inalienable right. Women still have a hard time giving orders because they have taken them for so long. Never fear, help is here.

Just treat him the way you wished someone had treated you.

1. Make sure he knows you are helpless without him.
2. Give him a correcting Selectric in a color to match his eyes.
3. Let him have his own imprinted memo pads.
4. Let him watch TV during the World Series.
5. Ask him how he's getting along with his roommate since the Jello in the bathtub misunderstanding.
6. Surprise him with hockey tickets.
7. If he comes in and hasn't shaved, don't ask him where he spent the night.
8. Treat him to lunch at the Athletic Club during National Secretaries Week.
9. Be sympathetic when he comes in red-eyed from a fight with his girlfriend.
10. Let him leave early because he has to see his urologist.

Quiz #1

Rate Your Office

The following questions are designed to help you determine whether your working environment is one that will lead you to the executive dining room or keep you forever brown-bagging it with the rest of the "support staff."

1. ***Your immediate superior***
    a. never seems to remember your name.
    b. refers to you as his "girl."
    c. takes your messages.

2. ***For Christmas last year you got***
    a. his wife's shopping list (she's too busy).
    b. asked to work overtime because you "didn't have a family."
    c. a big chunk of company stock.

3. ***When you told them you were pregnant***
    a. your boss said, "See, no sooner do we train them than they leave."
    b. they referred you to the nearest free clinic.
    c. they turned the men's gym into a day care center.

4. ***Last month when you had cramps***
    a. your boss suggested you see a psychiatrist.
    b. the men in your department compared stories about their wives.
    c. they closed the office for three days.

5. ***Lunch hours are***
    a. always 45 minutes.
    b. spent doing your turn at the switchboard.
    c. on your expense account.

6. ***Getting a cup of coffee means***
   a. making it yourself.
   b. going to the catering truck in the parking lot.
   c. having your boy bring it.

7. ***Vacations mean***
   a. wallpapering your bedroom.
   b. a visit to your cousin in Asbury Park, New Jersey.
   c. a month at the company condo in Acapulco.

8. ***You park your car***
   a. ten blocks away.
   b. you don't, you take the bus.
   c. in a reserved space by the door.

Scoring:
a = 1 point
b = 2 points
c = 3 points

21–24 points: Redecorate your office and join the pension plan. You should be here a long time.

14–20 points: Be of stout heart, learn what you can, and start updating your resume.

7–13 points: Call an executive placement service—TODAY.

0–6 points: Why, oh why are you in that place? Report these people to the Equal Rights Commission.

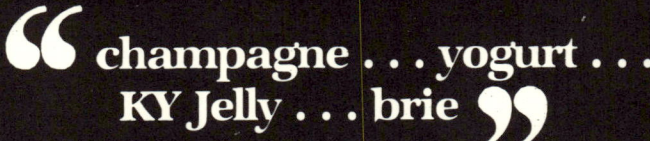

How to Be on Top at Home

3

Four Basic Household Hints*

*I*sn't it enough that you hold down a demanding job, dress like Lauren Hutton, and give parties that people talk about for weeks after? No, you have to be a super housekeeper, burning with desire for sparkling baseboards, gleaming floors, and crisp ironed sheets. *Men* may live like a herd of swine, but let *you* be caught with an unmopped floor and *you* are the one with the lazy, indulgent life-style.

The successful woman has learned a few simple tricks to maximize her image with a minimum of effort.

1. To alleviate refrigerator odor, keep an open bottle of Chanel No. 5 on the bottom shelf.
2. Entertain only after dusk, by candlelight. No one will be able to tell that the maid didn't show up.
3. If unexpected guests show up at your door and you didn't have time to take out the garbage, stick it in the vegetable bin of your refrigerator.†
4. If you have an overnight guest and forgot to change the sheets, put your down comforter on the floor in front of the fireplace—he'll think you're very romantic.

---

* If you need more than these, you have a more serious problem than we can help you with.
† The oven isn't a bad place, either.

Cold Storage

*H*ow many times have you been asked back to a man's apartment for drinks only to be served a can of flat beer accompanied by a bag of airline peanuts? Or had to breakfast on a handful of stale Cheerios and Lipton Instant Tea?

These experiences should have left you not only slightly nauseated, but firmly convinced that *your* refrigerator should be more than just a receptacle for half-eaten bananas and week-old coleslaw. You should be able to serve chic hors d'oeuvres on a moment's notice, whip up a gourmet super for two at 3:00 A.M., and provide the same service as your neighborhood drugstore . . . it's only a matter of selection.

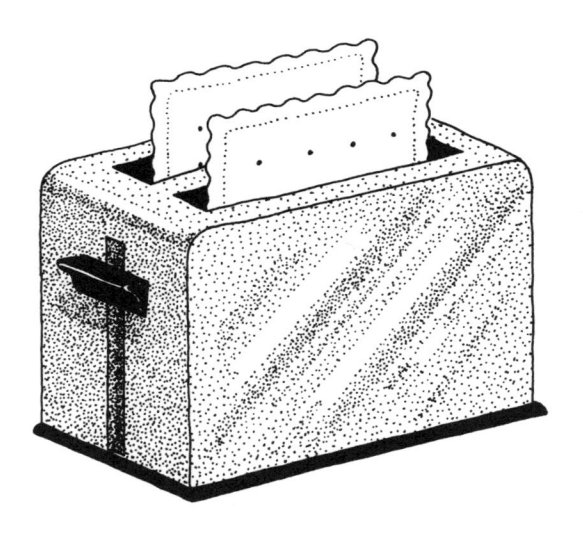

The Perfect Grocery List

BLW
- Champagne
- Stolichnaya in freezer
- Olives
- Artichoke Hearts
- KY jelly
- Dijon mustard
- Anchovies
- Ripe Brie
- Paté
- Polaroid film
- Silver martini glasses in freezer
- Heineken's
- Collagen elastin bee pollen vitamin E cream $80 oz.

CHAM
CHANEL no 5
ANCHOVIES
OLIV
ARTICHOKE HEART
RTICHOKE
EARTS
KY-J

What's in the Medicine Chest and . . .

There are certain unpleasant necessities of life that one must keep someplace, and generally that's the bathroom. However, the smart woman knows what to keep skillfully hidden away.

What's in the Medicine Chest

Christian Dior after shave

Unused toothbrush

Razor and fresh blades

Vitamin E

Trojans in assorted colors and sizes

Loofa

Imported massage oil

Scented bath oil

Candles

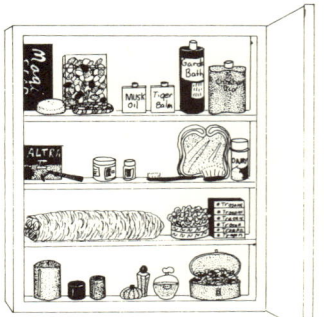

What's in a Shoe Box in the Back of Your Closet

Neet

Preparation H

Quell

Midol

Depilatory wax

Warts-Away

Vibrator

A lot of used toothbrushes

Hair color

Environmental Entertaining

*Y*ou don't have to worry about business entertaining, that's what expense accounts, posh restaurants, and pricey caterers are for.

But, what about those romantic evenings at home with just the two of you? Evenings when it's time to pull out all the stops and show no mercy.

Here are a few sure-fire suggestions for never-to-be-forgotten nights.

>   Champagne, oysters, and a jacuzzi
>
>   Vodka, caviar, and a fur rug
>
>   Chianti, pizza, and Pavorotti records
>
>   Hot sake, tempura, and a massage
>
>   Mateus Rose, shake 'n' bake, and satin sheets
>
>   Tequila, chili, and spurs

I Vant to Be Alone

At last. The unadulterated bliss of a free evening at home. No flying to Cleveland for a sales conference, no taking a client out to dinner, no obligatory visit to your parents, absolutely nothing that you *have* to do.

For many of us that's an excuse to cream our faces, eat a TV dinner, and schlump around in that ratty bathrobe we've had since college. Or you could:

> Whip up an avocado face masque in your Cuisinart.
>
> Polish your silver tea service.
>
> Repot two of your orchid plants.
>
> Gold leaf your guest bathroom faucets.
>
> Change the batteries in your vibrator.
>
> Rotate the art on your walls.
>
> Practice your pelvic exercises.
>
> Think of ten ways to get your boss's job.
>
> Plot revenge.
>
> Practice putting in your diaphragm in the dark.

Quiz #2

Rate Your Apartment

Your apartment may be the most revealing thing about you. Does yours invite thoughts of *Apartment Life* chic or early garage sale?

1. ***The couch in the living room***
   a. is a hide-a-bed (your mother comes to visit a lot).
   b. has broken springs from the six months you dated the hurdler.
   c. is a floor sample used in *Architectural Digest*.

2. ***The last time you had a problem in the bathroom it was because***
   a. the no-slip daisies in the bathtub mildewed.
   b. a bottle of nail polish spilled on the purple shag rug.
   c. you dropped your diamond studs down the sink.

3. ***The most used item in your kitchen is***
   a. an electric can opener.
   b. the garbage disposal.
   c. a Cuisinart.

4. ***If something spills in your living room***
   a. it doesn't matter—that's why you got a black shag rug.
   b. you just get a mop and sponge it off the linoleum.
   c. you call the insurance company—it's a $2,000 Oriental.

5. ***Your closet is***
   a. the shower rod in the bathroom.
   b. empty—everything is thrown on the bed.
   c. organized by color, season, and designer label.

6. *Your taste in art runs to*
    a. Keane paintings
    b. blowups of the pictures you took on your last vacation.
    c. good investments.

7. *The sheets on your bed are*
    a. black satin with an old whipped cream stain.
    b. Snoopy sheets your mother bought you in junior high.
    c. embroidered white cotton (the maid irons them).

8. *The reading on your night table is*
    a. *Soap Opera Digest.*
    b. Bruce Jenner's biography.
    c. Italian *Vogue.*

Scoring:
a = 1 point
b = 2 points
c = 3 points

24–18 points: You really must be earning the money if you can afford to live like this.

15–7 points: Have Goodwill come by, but don't be surprised if they look insulted.

6–0 points: How did you have the taste to buy this book? It must have been a gift.

On Top on the Road

*E*ver since they were old enough to say "vroom vroom," men have had a passionate relationship with their cars. Women, on the other hand, were supposed to drive a "sensible" car or be content to be a passenger in a "man's car" (i.e., sporty, powerful, and low-slung). No longer! Here's how you, too, can achieve the thrill of a five-speed and enjoy the throb of an overhead cam.

Do buy a Mercedes.

Don't hang a high school tassel on the mirror.

Do order custom upholstery.

Don't make it crushed velvet.

Do get a custom license plate.

Don't put your phone number on it.

Do get a cassette deck.

Don't play the Osmonds.

Do get a special paint job.

Don't make it metallic so it glows in the dark.

Do get a car phone.

Don't make it a princess.

Do put in a bar.

Don't serve Boone's Farm.

Do make sure it has a spacious back seat.

Don't use it.

Do have your own Mercedes mechanic.

Don't ask him what he did during World War II.

Do have a distinctive sounding horn.

Don't have it play "Lara's Theme."

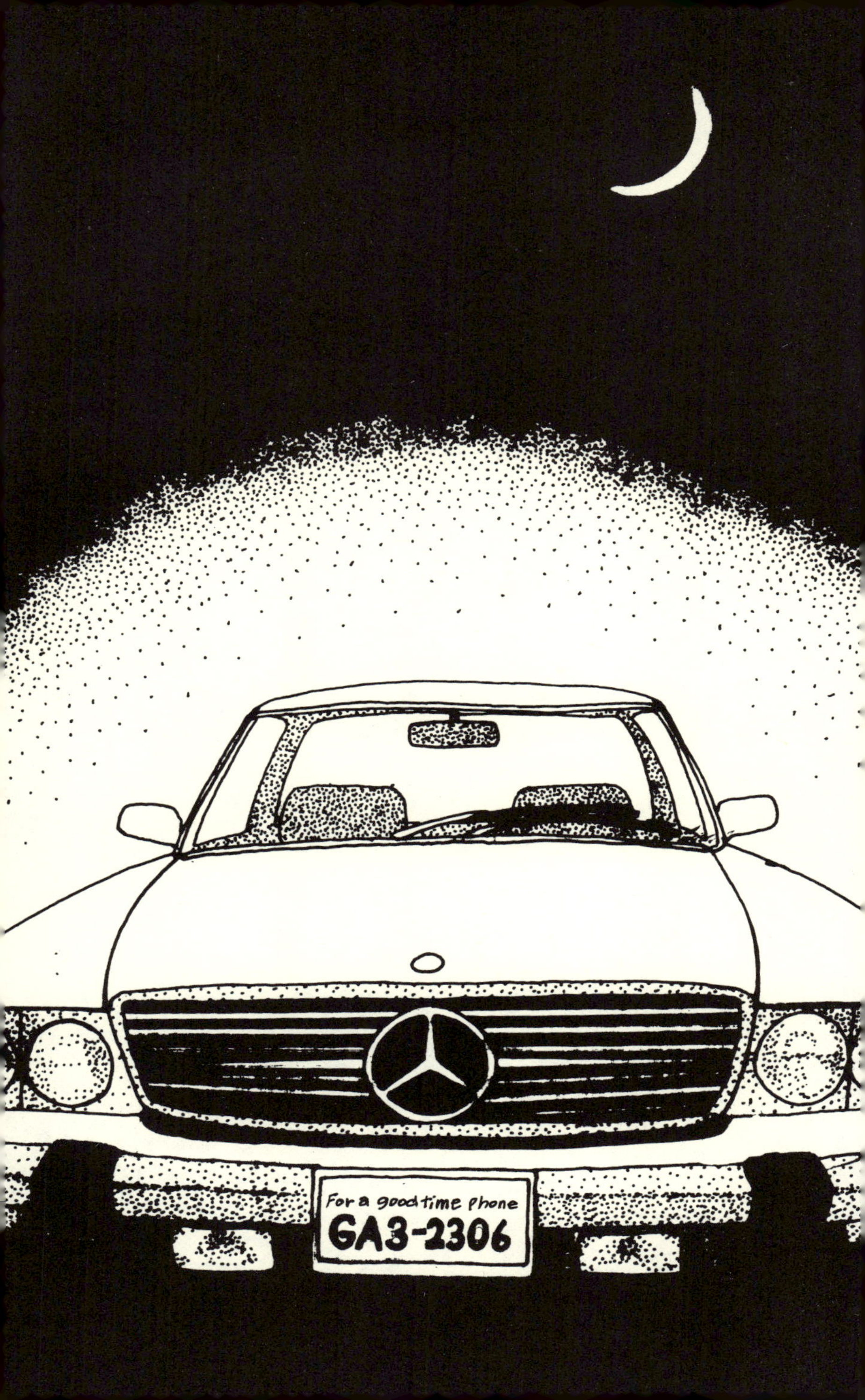
For a good time phone
GA3-2306

> **OFFENSIVE STATEMENT:** I don't know why you won't go to bed with me. I'm really good.
>
> **YOUR RESPONSE:** Practice a lot alone?

Staying on Top of Attacks from the Bottom

4

IF YOU CAN'T BEAT THEM...

CHANGE COMPANIES

Squelch 'Em!

No matter how hard you've worked to achieve the position of prosperity and respect you now enjoy, somebody will try to rain on your parade. Someone who loves to dampen spirits and feels it is his or her duty to "put you in your place." These delightful people can turn up anywhere—it could be your date, your best friend's husband, or even your very own sister. It eventually becomes necessary to remind them exactly where your place is. Above theirs.

OFFENSIVE STATEMENT: And who's the little lady?

YOUR RESPONSE: *Your new boss.*

OFFENSIVE STATEMENT: What's a nice girl like you doing in a place like this?

YOUR RESPONSE: *Undercover vice duty. You're under arrest.*

OFFENSIVE STATEMENT: Step aside, Miss. This is man's work.

YOUR RESPONSE: *Somebody need a urine sample in a Coke bottle?*

OFFENSIVE STATEMENT: I believe that keeping a home is a woman's most important job.

YOUR RESPONSE: *I agree. I kept the homes from my last three marriages.*

OFFENSIVE STATEMENT: What you need is a good lay.

YOUR RESPONSE: *I agree. It's boring having to teach all the time.*

OFFENSIVE STATEMENT: You're very articulate for a woman.

YOUR RESPONSE: *And you're very articulate for a baboon.*

OFFENSIVE STATEMENT: Are you one of those liberated women?

YOUR RESPONSE: *What gave me away? The assertive, assured way in which I told you to buzz-off?*

OFFENSIVE STATEMENT: It's too bad you never got married.

YOUR RESPONSE: *After your husband and I ended our affair I just threw myself into my work.*

OFFENSIVE STATEMENT: You've got great legs for a vice-president.

YOUR RESPONSE: *And you've got great taste for someone who's about to be unemployed.*

OFFENSIVE STATEMENT: I don't know why you don't want to go to bed with me. I'm really good.

YOUR RESPONSE: *Practice a lot alone?*

Who Asked You, Anyway?

From the time we were little girls somebody has been telling us what to do. First it was our parents, then our teachers, then our boyfriends or husbands, and always, our bosses. Women have been the recipients of more unasked-for advice than anyone. No one would dream of telling a man that "that shade of green does nothing for your complexion," but strangers on the street feel free to come up and tell you that you shouldn't carry a briefcase *and* a handbag.

Advice may be unavoidable, but taking it isn't. There are people who obviously should be ignored, like men over 21 who still live with their mothers, or anyone with a large transistor radio plastered to his ear. On the other hand, there are those who should be given consideration, such as IRS auditors and anyone with handcuffs on his briefcase.

Here are some ways to identify the two types of people you will come across in your life.

People Not to Take Seriously	People to Take Seriously
Bo Derek	The truck stop waitress who tells you about "life"
The lady trying to sell you a $60 facial	A ten-year-old who tells you you're fat
Men who fall in love on the first date	Your best friend when she hates the man you live with
Gay Talese	Masters and Johnson
The mechanic in "Middle-of-Nowhere," New Mexico who says you need a new water pump	Anyone who had four years of Latin in high school

Men who live with their mothers

Tennis opponents in tube tops

People who collect Keane paintings

Anybody who writes a "how-to" book

Men who still wear gold chains

Anyone who's been through est

Men who say "ciao"

Men bearing diamonds

Bjorn Borg

People who bequeath their collections to the Smithsonioan

Anybody who really knows "how-to"

❝ Do you find your eyes dropping to his crotch when he's trying to tell you something important? ❞

At Last, Men

5

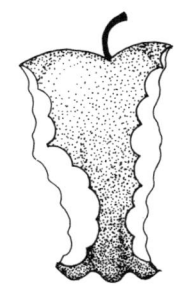

You Must Meet the Most Fascinating Men

"You're attractive and you've got a great job. You must meet the most fascinating men."

*T*his remark can be made at various times by your mother (who thinks meeting men is marrying men), your divorced sister in Fargo, your oldest friend, or the waitress at the local deli. The consensus is, you are first rate, so where are all those men who, *Cosmopolitan* assures you, come with being bright, intelligent, competent and perfumed? Here's a random sampling of what makes many successful women break out in hives.

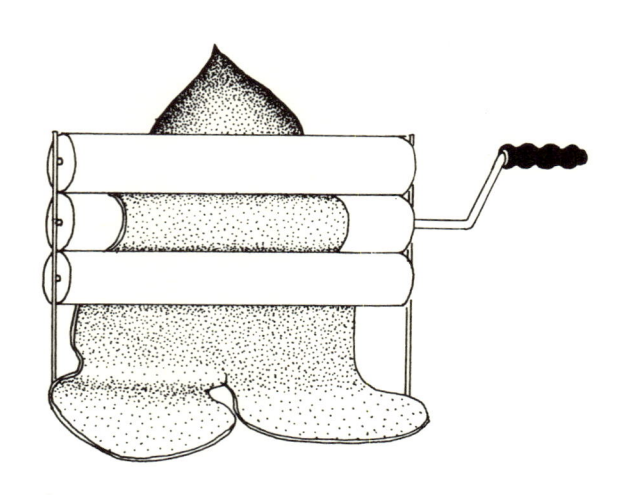

NAME:	*"Two Dot" Black*
HOW WE MET:	*In a hotel lobby while out of town on business.*
WHY I WENT OUT WITH HIM:	*Curiosity. Primal instinct.*
WHAT WE DID:	*Dinner. He called the maitre d' "boy" and me "honey." Drank Coors beer with the sole en croute.*
WHAT WE TALKED ABOUT:	*The speed limit in Wyoming, the whorehouse in Livingston, Montana, how many square miles he owned, how lucky I was to have met him.*
HOW IT ENDED:	*I finally changed my phone number.*

NAME:	*Paul Hansen*
HOW WE MET:	*Friend's wedding.*
HOW HE LOOKED:	*A "9."*
WHY I WENT OUT WITH HIM:	*Ph.D. in economics, prep school in Europe, spoke three languages.*
WHAT WE DID:	*Took me to dives to eat barbeque. Asked me to his ranch to paint a fence. Yelled at me for washing the paint off in a horse trough.*

WHAT WE TALKED ABOUT:	*His plans to corner the beefalo market.*
HOW IT ENDED:	*Disappeared with the $1,646.00 I lent him.*

NAME:	*David Kessler*
HOW WE MET:	*VIP Reception at a film festival.*
WHAT HE LOOKED LIKE:	*Bearded, cuddly, dark, arty.*
WHY I WENT OUT WITH HIM:	*He was a "talked about new film director." Lust.*
WHAT WE DID:	*Lots of white wine.*
WHAT WE TALKED ABOUT:	*His unrequited passion for the actress who left him, the sexual perversions of his last film's leading man, my hair (some sort of weird fetish).*
HOW IT ENDED:	*At the screening of his latest film. I fell asleep.*

NAME:	*Skip Reid*
HOW WE MET:	*Spotted him from afar, got a mutual friend to interest him in calling me.*
WHAT HE LOOKED LIKE:	*Skinny, buck-toothed, extremely tight clothing. Chemistry—what can I say?*

WHY I WENT OUT WITH HIM:	*Stage manager and TV director.*
WHAT WE DID:	*Went to innumerable quiche-butcher-block-hanging-plant restaurants, all with the same menu.*
WHAT WE TALKED ABOUT:	*God only knows.*
HOW IT ENDED:	*He stopped calling when his wife came back to town.*

NAME:	*Ronald Collins*
HOW WE MET:	*While eating at Harry's Bar & Grill in New York.*
WHAT HE LOOKED LIKE:	*Adonis. 6'3", blond, blue eyes, 35-year-old aristocrat in an expensive blue suit. Took me ten minutes to realize he was talking to me.*
WHY I WENT OUT WITH HIM:	*Tenor in the San Francisco Opera.*
WHAT WE DID:	*Went to my apartment mostly.*
WHAT WE TALKED ABOUT:	*How fabulous he was, how well-traveled he was, how cultured he was, how he could teach a hick like me to be sophisticated.*
HOW IT ENDED:	*Herpes.*

Where to Look

We have already discussed this problem and the caliber of men one unfortunately meets most of the time. As a woman on her way (or already) up, the problem is compounded. Here are some guidelines garnered from our friendly travel agent and from personal research.

1. Join the Admiral's Club.
2. Take New York to Los Angeles American flight 21.
3. Go to the Sotheby Parke-Bernet auctions.
4. Hang out at Brooks Brothers.
5. Buy your sporting gear at Abercrombie & Fitch.
6. Have a box seat at your local polo club.
7. Get a seat on the stock exchange.
8. Join the Petroleum Club.
9. Only have lunch at places where the entrees start at $9.50.
10. Buy your own 40-foot sailboat.
11. Back a Broadway play.
12. Buy a football team. (If you're over 5 feet 10 inches, buy a basketball team.)
13. Invest in a vineyard.
14. Learn to speak Arabic.
15. Sponsor a Formula One Grand Prix car.
16. Learn to play baccarat.

The Bicoastal, Out-of-Town, "Always-on-the-Road" Relationship

One problem posed by rising to levels of corporate responsibility is that you will probably have to travel a great deal. And so will the men you meet. There may be sensual, late night meetings at foggy airports and the sweet reminders offered by the handsoaps swiped from the last hotel weekend, but there are also going to be lots of phone calls trying to arrange how and where to meet between trips to Baltimore. Before you embark on such a complicated affair, perhaps you should consider:

Advantages	Disadvantages
It's easier to stick to your 850-calorie a day diet.	You're too weak to get on the plane.
You only have to shave under your arms the night before you meet.	Terrible razor burn.
He doesn't see you wearing the same outfits.	He thinks you squander money on clothes.
Late night phone calls are very romantic.	You're not always alone—the phone wakes Harry.
You can mess up his house and not clean it up.	He can mess up your house and not clean it up.
He travels so much that stews give him special attention.	The special attention takes place in their hotel rooms.
He writes letters.	His secretary types them.
He doesn't know about Harry.	You don't know about Sally.

The 1980s Male

Before you make the commitment to share the rent, better take a long, hard look at what you might be pairing up with. After the first glow of passion (those green eyes, that body, that condo in Aspen) has passed, he may not be all that you deserve.

The American male is divided into two personality types. If you find yourself with Type A, don't let him get away. If you've become involved with Type B, disentangle yourself *immediately* and ask yourself why you ever got involved with such an oaf.

A

Is supportive of your career.

Is able to amuse himself if you're late meeting him.

Makes a great soufflé.

Takes you out to celebrate your promotion.

Encourages you to be open and honest with your feelings.

Shares the business section with you at breakfast.

Makes sure you're included in the conversation at dinner with his boss.

Gets to know your neighbors.

Laughs at your jokes.

For your birthday he buys you a new squash racket and a sheer black negligee.

When it's cold he doesn't care if you wear socks to bed.

B

Still refers to his secretary as his "girl."

Sulks and tells you that the relationship will never work, 'till you don't.

Is sure all chefs are "queers."

Thinks you're overpaid.

Accuses you of being emotionally aggressive.

Hands you the women's page.

Suggests you help in the kitchen.

Leaves at 4:00 A.M. so he won't ruin your reputation.

Thinks funny women are vulgar.

Gives you a sewing machine and a month of free lessons.

Claims your career has made you frigid.

How to Buy a Man

Perhaps you don't want marriage or commitment at this point in your life. Your career takes most of your energy, and you like it that way. But there is still the need for some good unwholesome fun with a well-built creature of the male persuasion. The easiest and best solution is the straightforward approach. Buy one.

Men have done this with women for years, apparently to their profound satisfaction. If you decide on this course of action, do not allow mere "chemistry" to get in the way of intelligent selection. This is a major purchase and requires at least as much thought and research as you would put into buying a car. First, settle on a body type, decide on color and available options, and get down to the basic questions.

Have you taken him home for a test drive?

Did you look under the hood?

Does he start on a cold morning?

Does he turn over easily?

Is he one of those fancy Italian jobs that's constantly in the shop?

Has he had more than one owner?

Can he really hug the curves?

Does he make a lot of noise while running?

Did you get underneath and check the chassis?

Is he good for the long haul or only short hops?

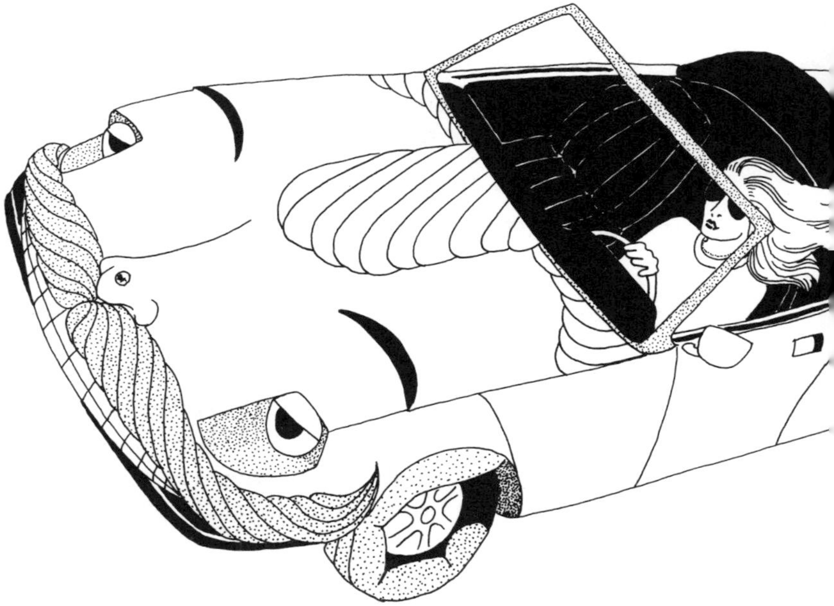

What to Say to Your Mother Who Thinks You Should Get Married and Have Somebody Take Care of You

There is absolutely *nothing* new you can say to your mother that hasn't been said by countless women before you, with greater or lesser degrees of vehemence. It is simply impossible for some ladies of a certain generation to comprehend that you can take care of yourself, that you love your career, and that you desire a variety of men.

Keep this list by your telephone for those times she calls and you are caught with your excuses down.*

> I will, I will, as soon as I finish my book.
>
> You wouldn't want me to marry just anybody, would you? Look what happened to Aunt Helen!
>
> All the good ones are taken.
>
> I'm only 33, I have time.
>
> Let me get this career business out of my system first.
>
> I will, as soon as he gets a divorce.
>
> Helen Gurley Brown didn't get married until she was 37 and look what a terrific guy she got.
>
> I met the most divine man. . . . (Sometimes you just have to let her think there's someone in your life. After a few years you can say it just didn't work out.)

---

* If you have any new "mother placaters" the authors would appreciate hearing from you.

Quiz #3

How to Tell if You're Being a Female Chauvinst Pig

There has been a lot of talk about male chauvinist pigs in the last few years, but women too, can fall into the trap of sexual stereotyping. If you answer yes to more than three of the following questions, don't be surprised when your husband starts spending all of his spare time in a consciousness raising group, your secretary puts your call sheets through the shredder, or your boyfriend takes a male lover.

Do you think all airline stewards are easy?

Do you tell him that what he needs is a good lay?

Do you laugh when he asks for a committed relationship?

Do you make your "boy" keep score while you and the women from the office play hardball?

Do you make him do the dishes while you discuss business with your guests?

Do you make him do all the shopping because you "never have the time"?

Do you ask him to wear tight pants so you can see his buns better?

Have you said, "Just look gorgeous and keep quiet"?

Do you hate his emotional outbursts during a full moon?

Do you find your eyes dropping to his crotch when he is trying to tell you something important?

A Puzzlement

See if you can find all the animals hidden in the puzzle below. The answers to the questions can be found backwards, forwards, across, up and down, and sideways. We'll give you the first one.

B	Q	N	T	S	O	N	L
G	E	R	M	P	N	E	M
M	J	K	E	B	W	M	Z
X	Y	O	N	E	M	A	I
U	N	S	M	T	M	M	U
M	E	N	M	E	J	E	K
A	M	E	P	I	N	N	N
G	N	I	M	E	N	S	R

1. Of Mice and _____ .
2. The opposite of women.
3. Sex is the only thing they are good for.
4. In sports they express happiness by patting each other's rear ends.
5. The only animals on Earth who believe they are always right.
6. Fools for flattery.
7. Big boobs make them act like that.
8. These creatures frequently find security by banding together in "clubs" named after fierce animals.
9. Cars hold mystical power over them.
10. Animals who sometimes think with their reproductive organs.
11. Have been known to talk about themselves entire evenings *even after everyone has gone to sleep.*

What Do All These Objects Have in Common?

Coffee
A man
A cat

They can keep you awake at night.

Candy
A man
Flowers

Your mother would be thrilled if you brought them home.

Cab driver
A man
Snail

It is hard to get their attention.

Horses
A man
Weather

Don't bet on them.

Money
A man
Keys

They can open doors for you.

Women Who Proved That Maybe it Isn't So Bad to Stay Single

Marquessa De Sade

Mrs. "Bride" of Frankenstein

Anyone married to Henry VIII

Guinevere

Juliet

Josephine

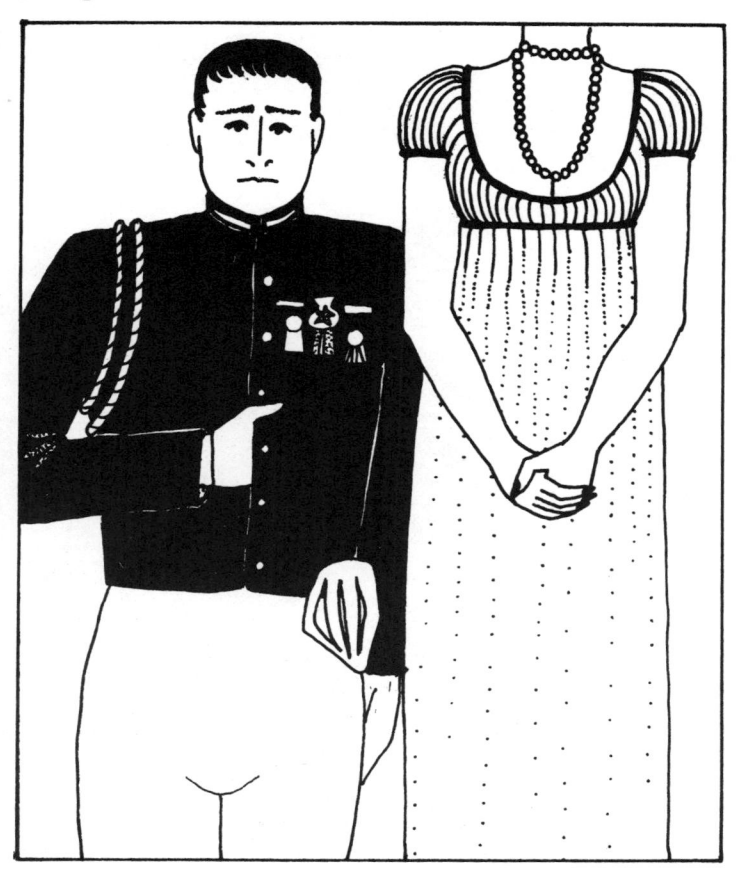

> "A perfect way to spend an evening is to get smashed with the girls and eye young men in tight jeans"

If You Can't Join 'Em—Beat 'Em

6

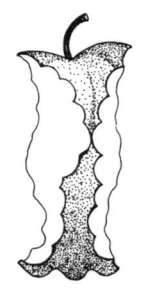

Recreation

For as long as there has been free time there has been recreation, and men have cornered the market. They say things like, "We work hard, we play hard," or "All work and no play makes Jack a dull boy." Well, what about Jill? She schlepped that bucket up the hill, too. If we were to believe TV, men find their rewards in bars comparing beer, sailing on the high seas, and smoking cigarettes on horseback, while women need only the thrill of a sparkling toilet bowl to make their day.

Give me a break!

We, too, like to sit around in our underwear and watch the tube. We, too, can vent our hostilities smashing a tennis racket down someone's throat.

They don't have to teach us a thing about goofing-off. We know that one of the perfect ways to spend an evening is to get smashed with the girls and eye young men in tight jeans.

How to Be on Top of Your Leisure Time

Drink beer and compare the rear ends of football players.

Take that sweet young thing from the art department away from it all for the weekend. Give him a raise for being so "nice."

Go to the gym and lure an unsuspecting jock into a game of racquetball. Beat him unmercifully.

Have your chauffeur drive you to the car wash in your Rolls. Watch the men turn green.

When your boyfriend wants to spend the weekend watching the Super Bowl with the "boys," fly yourself and the "girls" to the game and watch it from the 50-yard line. Wave to the TV cameras.

Sportsperson

Sportsman (sports'men): A man who abides by the rules of a contest and accepts victory or defeat graciously.

The above is the dictionary definition of a sportsman.

Sportswoman (sports'wo men): A woman who abides by the rules of a contest and graciously lets the man win.

The above is the unwritten definition of a sportswoman.

Most of us grew up hearing, "Now, honey, let the boys win." Fortunately, we didn't listen or we wouldn't be where we are today, but we probably were affected in smaller ways. How many times have you let him believe it was beginner's luck? Or listened quietly as he erroneously explained the rules to you? Or served over after he called your ace out?

We don't have to play that way any longer. If they can't face the truth, that's *their* problem. Just remember that sportspersonship *does* include that "accepting victory graciously" part. Don't gloat. (Well, not too much, anyway.)

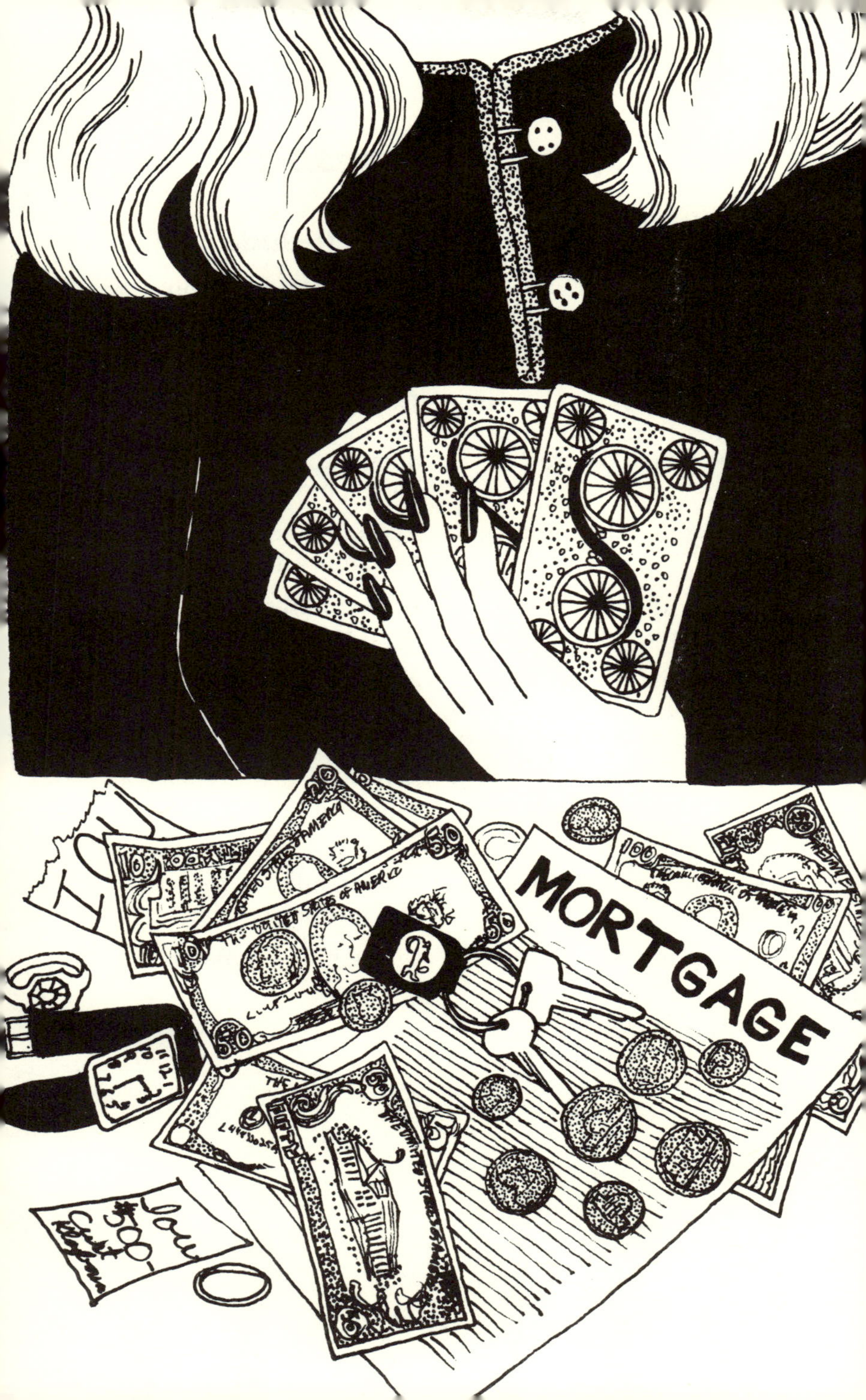
MORTGAGE

Sportspersonship

Does not include

Letting the men win

Watching him show off in the gym.

Accepting a few betting dollars from him when he takes you to the track

Asking for a handicap.

Sitting quietly while he explains the rules to you.

Pretending to be thrilled when he shows you how to flip him with a judo move.

Having him give you a crib sheet with what hand beats what in poker.

Settling for "Old Bess" on the trail ride.

Letting him serve softly.

Does include

Letting your boss win.

Lifting the barbell off of him after he has collapsed.

Paying his gambling debts out of your winnings and allowing him to pay you back a little each week.

Accepting one and beating his pants off.

Letting him play when the team is ahead.

Not seriously injuring him.

Accepting his mortgage as collateral.

Taking him to the chiropractor the next day.

Giving him a rematch.

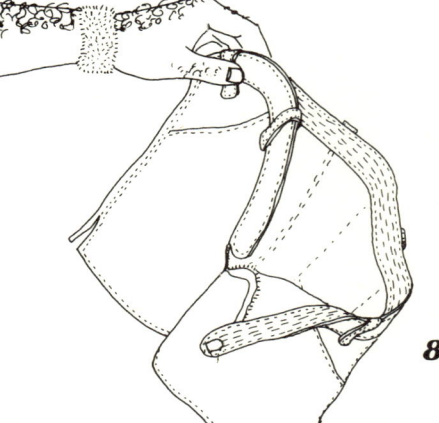

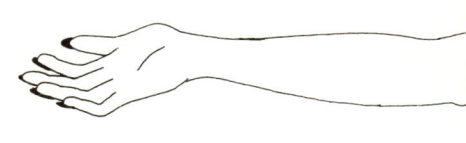

Nobody Likes a Bitch

God knows, you didn't get where you are today by keeping your opinions to yourself or being a soft touch. As any relatively successful fool knows, clawing your way to the top involves a bit of aggressive behavior, a firm grasp on intimidation techniques, and even outright ruthlessness from time to time.

But it's no fun being on top if everyone is drooling in anticipation of your fall. So watch carefully for the signs that you may have become a little heavy-handed in dealing with others.

> When you go to brush a lock of hair out of his face he protects his eyes.
>
> Everyone stops talking when you walk through the office.
>
> People never look you in the eyes.
>
> Your hairdresser lets you cut your own bangs.
>
> He locks himself in the bathroom during an argument.
>
> People send you apology notes when they sneeze in your presence.
>
> No one *ever* makes an improper advance.
>
> Your best friends call you Ms. _____ .
>
> You go through fifty-two secretaries a year.
>
> You return from vacation fifteen pounds heavier and nobody mentions it.
>
> Your last three boyfriends joined a monastery.

"You know you've made it when you ask to see his legs."

You've Made It!

7

The Nine Most Important People in a Successful Woman's Life

Stockbroker

Hairdresser

Foreign car mechanic

Exercise teacher

Secretary

Dressmaker

Wine merchant

Florist

Dry cleaner

A Warning!

**Ten Rotten Things that Can Happen
Just When You Thought that Being
Rich, Beautiful, Successful,
Admired, and Fabulously Well-adjusted
Would Solve All Your Problems:**

1. Your boyfriend borrows your new Mercedes and totals it.
2. The filter backs up in your pool.
3. The air conditioner in your wine cellar breaks down.
4. You find your maid feeding the dog out of a Baccarat fruit bowl.
5. Your Malibu beach house is washed away.
6. Your Russian wolfhound relieves himself on your new Oriental carpet.
7. The land you bought as a tax write-off gushes oil.
8. Your company's chief competitor offers you a job at double your salary creating a moral crisis.
9. You find out the Rembrandt sketch you got such a good deal on is a forgery.
10. The captain of your yacht is arrested for running cocaine in from Central America.

Quiz #4

How to Know if You've Made It

1. ***The last time someone phoned you at home on a Saturday night, you were:***
   a. Flying back from Friday night.
   b. Watching a Mary Tyler Moore Show rerun.
   c. Finishing off a Sara Lee cheesecake.

2. ***You carry your makeup in:***
   a. Your briefcase.
   b. The pocket of your jeans.
   c. A Book-of-the-Month Club tote.

3. ***Your last vacation was:***
   a. At home with your parents.
   b. A group tour of Civil War battlefields.
   c. Having your tush lifted.

4. ***The last time you saw Paris was:***
   a. The movie starring Elizabeth Taylor.
   b. On a backdrop at your senior class play.
   c. Never—your European office is in Geneva.

5. ***Your last dinner party was ruined because:***
   a. Henry Kissinger brought two extra women.
   b. You forgot to drain the tuna for the tuna-noodle casserole.
   c. Your dog upset the TV trays.

6. ***The White House is:***
   a. The hamburger stand on 10th Street.
   b. Where you had dinner last week.
   c. Your grandmother's.

7. ***Having your hair done means:***
   a. Peroxide and Q-tips.
   b. A quick stopover in N.Y.
   c. The circus is coming to town.

Correct Answers:

1(a) 2(a) 3(c) 4(c) 5(a) 6(b) 7(b)

6–7 correct: Congratulations. Write and tell us how you did it.

3–5 correct: Don't give up now. You're going in the right direction.

1–2 correct: Go directly to the yellow pages, look under Guidance Counselors and make an appointment.

DON'T SEND A BOY

TO DO A MAN'S JOB.

. . . . . .

SEND A WOMAN

You know you've made it when...

you're the one on top.

you give him an allowance.

the wine steward gives you the cork.

you have to take his credit cards away.

You know you've made it when....

the M.D. is after your name.

you ply him with drink.

you have to explain the rules to him.

the **Wall Street Journal** *is delivered to you.*

You know you've made it when...

the family relocates with you.

he has to pick the kids up after school.

You know you've made it when...

nobody keeps track of when you get back from lunch.

you always get your man.

your book is more scandalous than his.

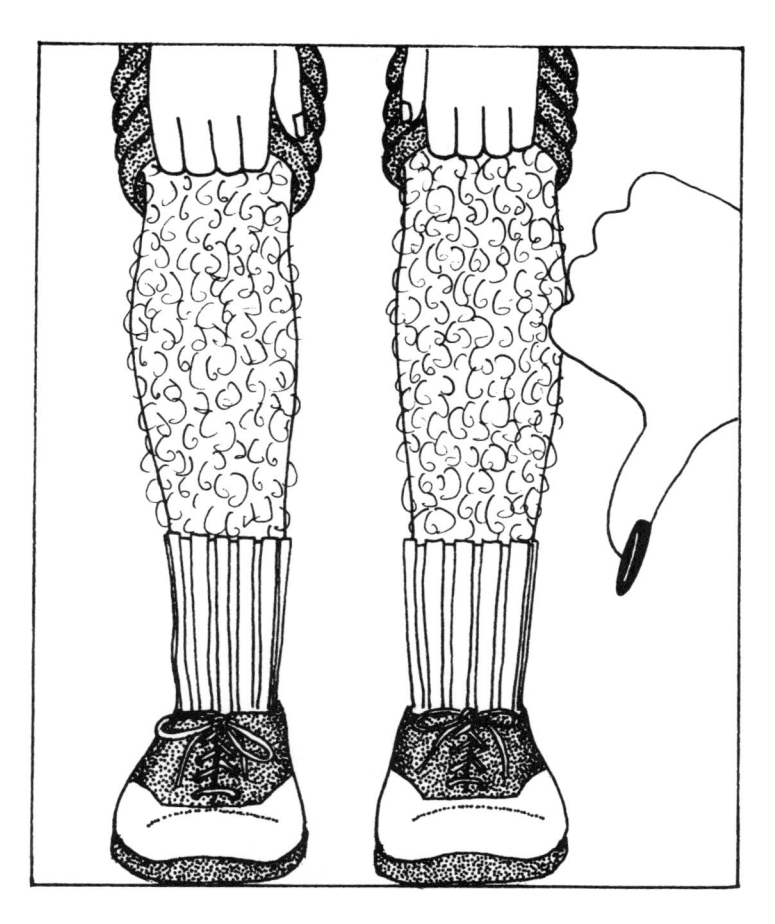

you ask to see his legs.

You know you've made it when...

your company subscribes to Ms.

you're the one who checks out the funny noises.

You know you've made it when...

nobody is surprised you got elected.

the needlepoint pillows are his.

they treat you like one of the boys.

you're the one working late at the office.

You know you've made it when...

you get a good table because the headwaiter was a great one-night stand.

the semi is yours.

You know you've made it when...

you don't have to know how to use the coffee machine.

your uniforms are the same.

they're picketing to get into your club.

you make them blush.

you can take him away from it all.

the token is a white male.

there's a Tampax machine in the executive washroom.

Can You Do It Again?

*F*ind your way through the pitfalls of growing up a woman and come out on top.

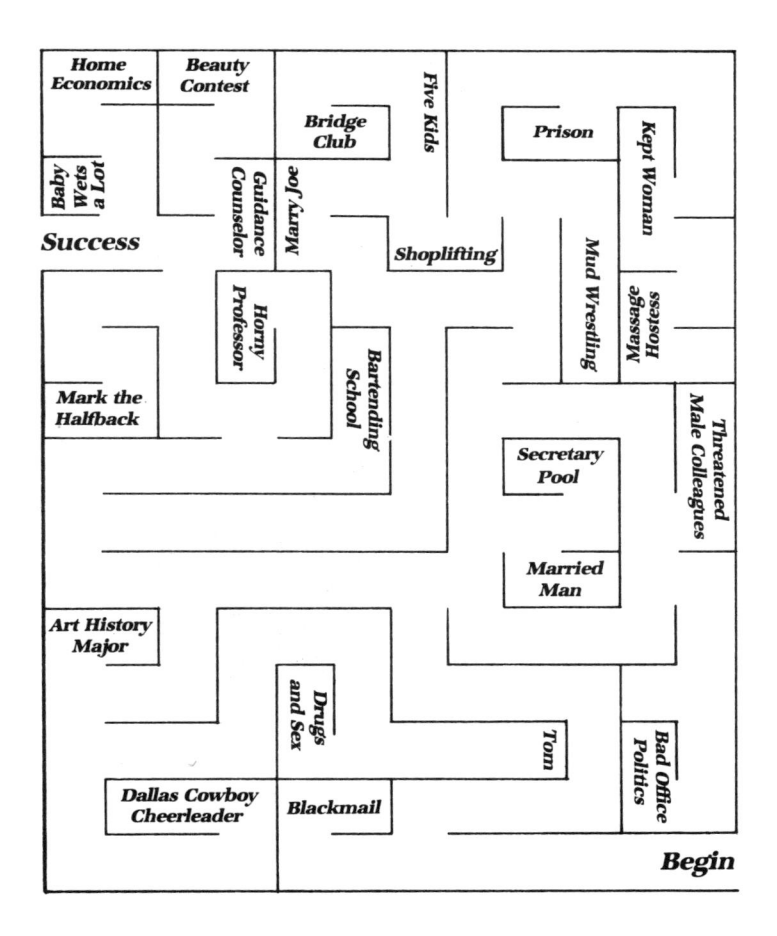

Home Economics	Beauty Contest		Five Kids		Prison	Kept Woman
Baby Wets a Lot	Guidance Counselor	Bridge Club				
Success		Marry Joe	Shoplifting		Mud Wrestling	Massage Hostess
	Horny Professor		Bartending School			
Mark the Halfback						Threatened Male Colleagues
				Secretary Pool		
				Married Man		
Art History Major						
		Drugs and Sex		Tom	Bad Office Politics	
	Dallas Cowboy Cheerleader	Blackmail				
						Begin

125

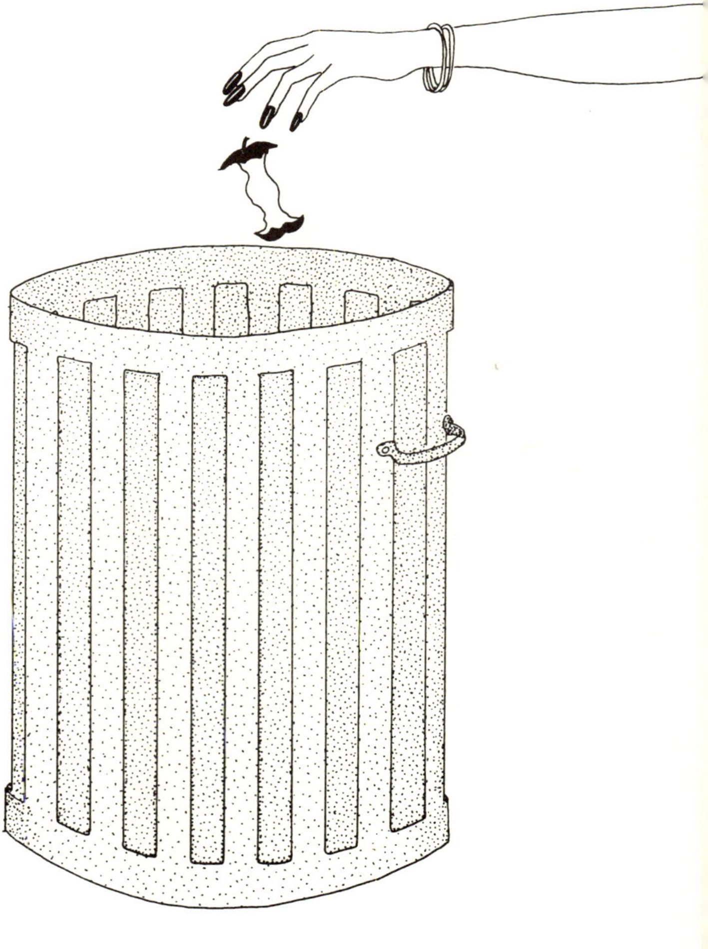

About the Authors

Mary Lou Brady *spends too many weekends in Las Vegas and for the past twenty years has indulged in a trombone player fetish. This flaming redhead works as a Publicity Director for a firm that wishes to remain anonymous.*

Lucinda Dyer *reads too much and exercises to excess. She has a passionate attachment to country western music, buckwheat groats, and Malcolm Muggeridge. Her leisure time is spent in quest of the perfect corn chip.*

Sara Parriott *is the author of* Sex Doesn't Count When, Calories Don't Count When, *and* You Don't Have to Exercise When. *She is soon to become a major motion picture in collaboration with her husband Joe and their cat Chuck.*

All three authors live in Los Angeles.

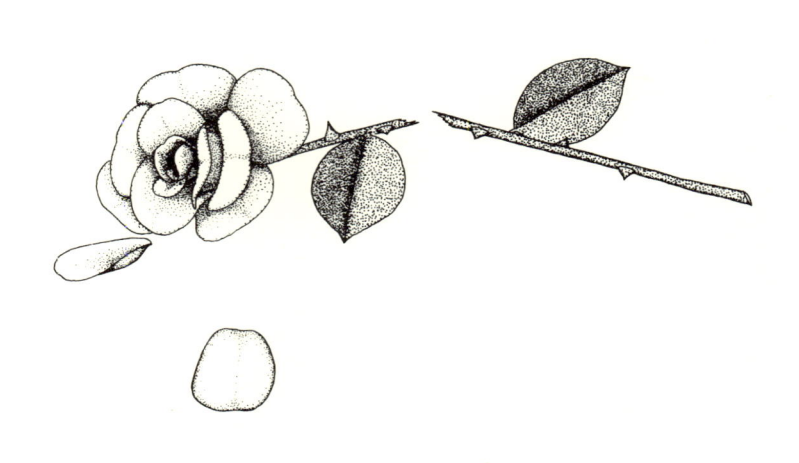